# Halfway to the Future

# Halfway to the Future

*Reflections on the Global Condition*

On the Occasion of the
25th Anniversary of the Tellus Institute

2001

COPYRIGHT 2001 © TELLUS INSTITUTE
ISBN: 0-9712418-0-5

*Published by*

TELLUS INSTITUTE
11 ARLINGTON STREET
BOSTON, MA 02116-3411 USA
WEBSITE: WWW.TELLUS.ORG
EMAIL: INFO@TELLUS.ORG

*Photographic credits*
PAGES vi AND 2, COURTESY OF NASA;
PAGE 34, COURTESY OF THE UNITED NATIONS, AND
PAGE 44, COURTESY OF STONE/DAVID HANOVER

*Illustration credits*
PAGES 15, 20, AND 33 BY JOYCE WESTON;
PAGE 39 BY PILLE BUNELL; PAGE 46 © MICHAEL MIRACLE

BOOK DESIGN BY JOYCE WESTON

 PRINTED ON RECYCLED PAPER

# Contents

Preface vii

Planetary Turbulence 3

The Challenge of Climate Change 9

Water in a Thirsty World 19

The End of Waste 27

Sustainability and the New Agenda 37

Our Grandchildren's Bequest 45

Acknowledgments 53

About the Tellus Institute 55

# Preface

What a difference twenty-five years can make. In 1976, a group of scientists formed the Tellus Institute as a not-for-profit organization focused on environmental research and policy. The young institute took up many key issues of the time — energy development, nuclear power and pollution — blending commitments to scientific rigor, environmental preservation and social equity. Tellus offered fresh perspectives that resonated with growing concerns about the character of economic development, the state of the environment and the erosion of social cohesion. Soon its program expanded to address the changing national and global agendas on environment and development. Tellus conducted projects all over North America and the world, forming a long and close partnership with first the Beijer Institute in Sweden and then its descendant, the Stockholm Environment Institute.

The story of Tellus has unfolded in the context of staggering changes around it. The very vocabulary that describes our research program today — sustainable development, climate change, eco-efficiency, globalization, electricity deregulation, information technology — was not even part of the environmental lexicon in 1976. The forces that are radically reshaping the world have also enlarged our vision. The issues we address have become more complex, our time horizon has lengthened from years to many decades and our perspective has broadened to include a global panorama. This evolution of the environment and development research program has tracked the deepening interconnectedness, uncertainty and globalization of the world itself.

Few of us have the luxury of stepping back from the hectic pace of our lives to take the long view in reflecting on our remarkable moment on Earth. At Tellus, we have used the milestone of our twenty-fifth anniversary as an opportunity for such a meditation. With the strong wind of global change at our backs, we come to the conviction that a major new era of world history has begun to take shape over recent decades. The fates of economies, cultures and communities are increasingly bound together by global commerce, communication and politics. The human disruption of the natural environment has grown to planetary scales. This emerging era — the planetary phase of civilization — is transforming both the Earth and ourselves.

> A major new era of world history has begun to take shape over recent decades.

The process of global transformation has been launched, but its ultimate direction has yet to be determined. The character of global society several decades from now is fundamentally uncertain. Will it be good, bad or ugly? Optimists find a basis for hope, and pessimists reasons for apprehension, as they observe unfolding events through the prisms of their world views. What is clear is that there is yet time to infuse global development with humanistic and ecological principles. The key is our ability to gain new insights, commit to new values and take common actions to create more harmonious conditions for life on Earth. What we do in the next twenty-five years — as citizens, scientists, communities and nations — is critical to our future, and in that sense we are halfway to the future.

# Halfway to the Future

# Planetary Turbulence

HISTORY SEEMS TO BE IN fast-forward mode. Images flicker by of technological, economic and cultural change. We watch the world grow vastly more complex as a global economy takes shape. A revolution in information technology unfolds before our eyes, changing our lives and speeding the spread of dominant cultural paradigms. Important new actors — transnational corporations, international institutions and a global civil society — take the stage to shape the unfolding drama. Unexpected fault lines of conflict appear across the geo-political landscape. An impoverished global majority, left behind by the new global economy, clamor ever more loudly for equity and participation. All the while, alarming reports of environmental degradation grow more frequent and more urgent.

These are turbulent times. As we live them, we cannot easily discern the historic theme that unifies these diverse phenomena. But with a long view, one defining feature of our era comes into focus — the human transformation of nature and society has reached a global scale. A tightening web of environmental, economic and social interactions binds nations, regions and communities into a single Earth system. The dynamics of the global whole increasingly govern the behavior of its parts. Civilization has entered its planetary phase.

The multiple strands of global change are part of a unitary transformation. The expansion of markets, the spread of consumerism and the alteration of the biosphere reinforce one another to accelerate global interdependence. At the same time, this process creates counter-tendencies to challenge the ascendancy of market-driven globalization. The traditionalist reaction resists the Americanization of world culture. A crisis of governance looms as the borderless economy eludes the authority of nation-states and invades communities. The flow of global "bads" rises — pollution, narcotics, arms, disease and terrorism — along with the increased trade of economic goods. Many nations struggle against internal disintegration and grinding poverty. Globally connected environmental and social justice movements oppose heedless economic growth and seek an alternative model of development. The character of the planetary future is contested.

> Globally connected environmental and social justice movements oppose heedless economic growth and seek an alternative model of development.

The historical roots of planetary civilization lie in the inexorable process of growth and transformation launched by the industrial revolution. Some two centuries ago, Western society transcended the stasis of traditional society, unleashing a chain reaction of technological, institutional and cultural change. Industrial capitalism liberated latent human potential for acquisition, innovation and competition. The scientific and industrial revolutions reinforced each other in a process of exponential change. A new entrepreneurial class — in the business of profit maximization, capital investment and expanded production — responded to and fostered a widening spiral of wants and needs. This expanding system engulfed communities in its midst and societies on its periphery. The long journey to globalization had begun.

The productive might of industrial capitalism brought unprecedented prosperity, but often at terrible human cost. While a new elite enjoyed the affluence of the industrial system, masses of people were impoverished by it. The market and factory systems displaced traditional livelihoods, communities and values, consigning the uprooted to a new kind of urban squalor. Basic protections and amenities — decent shelter, health and nutrition — were a privilege of affluence, not a right of all. In response, oppositional movements won concessions for better wages and working conditions, democratic enfranchisement, freedom and opportunity. Yet, to this day, the battle between rights and privileges remains central to political debates.

> The future will be defined by how two global crises are addressed — ecological degradation and extreme poverty.

The legacy of the industrial era is complex and contradictory. Its culmination is the planetary phase of human development, which unfolds before us in a frenzy of change. We inherit the capacity to eradicate the scourge of human deprivation, but the world remains mired in poverty and inequality. We have the scientific knowledge and command the technological wizardry to harmonize economics with ecology, but lack the institutions and political will. We are offered the historical opportunity to build a culture of peace, social renewal and self-realization, but lack the necessary breadth and depth of vision. Our global condition is rife with both opportunity and predicament.

To a large extent, the future will be defined by how two global crises — ecological degradation and extreme poverty — are addressed. The human impact on the environment is becoming progressively more complex, global and interconnected. Population pressure, bioaccumulation of toxic materials, degradation of ecosystems and soaring use of nonrenewable resources threaten to damage the planet's natural systems beyond their assimilative capacities. As developing nations emulate Western-style consumption patterns, the human footprint on nature grows ever larger. Meanwhile, two billion people confront chronic poverty and disenfranchisement, vulnerable to environmental, economic and political shocks.

> We have time and opportunity to envision and fashion a positive planetary transition over the coming decades.

In these early years of a new century, we have crossed the doorstep and entered the anteroom of a planetary world. But amidst the current tumult and uncertainty, no one can predict the structure of global society that lies ahead. The world could become more inclusive or more pernicious, more harmonious or more wanton, more civilized or more barbaric. Some who view events through a pessimistic filter can find validation of dark premonitions in the culture of complacency, myopia and selfishness that seems so ubiquitous. Yet the future remains open, subject to the choices people make in their daily lives, in their communities and as global citizens. Hope finds its foundation in the conviction that we have time and opportunity to envision and fashion a positive planetary transition over the coming decades.

# The Challenge of Climate Change

PERHAPS NO ISSUE better epitomizes the new planetary predicament than the human alteration of the Earth's climate. Throughout history the climate appeared as an autonomous force influencing our fragile endeavors. Only in the last two decades have we become aware of the fragility of the climate system itself. Climate change binds the human community in a common destiny. Its causes and consequences are complex and global — so must be the solution.

The Earth would be a frozen mass without the naturally occurring warming of the "greenhouse effect." Minute amounts of atmospheric gases capture some of the solar energy that the Earth radiates back towards space. But since the industrial revolution, the concentration of these greenhouse gases has increased substantially, due to human activity. Atmospheric carbon dioxide, the most important greenhouse gas, has increased by 30 percent to a level unprecedented in hundreds of millennia. Over the past century, global warming of about one degree Fahrenheit has paralleled the gradual buildup of greenhouse gases. The 1990s were the warmest decade of the millennium; as glaciers receded, the Antarctic ice shelf splintered and extreme weather events became more frequent.

Unfortunately, this may be only the prelude. With growing populations and expanding economies based on energy from fossil fuels, carbon dioxide emissions could triple by the end of the century. A recent report from the Intergovernmental Panel on Climate Change finds that average global temperatures could rise by over 10 degrees Fahrenheit. Both the historical record and scientific analysis suggest that global warming could have severe impacts on the Earth's climate and ecological systems. The hydrological cycle would intensify, increasing the incidence and severity of droughts, floods and hurricanes. Habitats would be altered, further threatening biodiversity. Tropical diseases such as malaria and dengue fever would likely spread northward and to higher elevations. Rising sea levels would inundate low-lying coastal areas and magnify sea storms.

> The climate system could shift abruptly when pushed beyond critical thresholds.

Such impacts may not evolve gradually. The pre-historic ice core record offers evidence of quite rapid climate change. As greenhouse gases accumulate, the climate system could shift abruptly when pushed beyond critical thresholds that cannot be precisely known in advance. Incremental change could trigger feedbacks that ripple through the climate system, amplifying and accelerating the process of climate destabilization. We can identify some of the possibilities — realignment of ocean currents, the loss of carbon-absorbing forests and the massive release of methane from the arctic or deep-ocean sediments. As human activity pushes the climate into novel conditions, dangerous surprises cannot be ruled out.

There is wide scientific consensus on the basic character of the problem and the reality of a "human fingerprint" on the

# THE CHALLENGE OF CLIMATE CHANGE

climate system. But the complexity of climate change makes it difficult to predict the precise timing and magnitude of its impacts. This leads some to advocate postponing action until further research reduces scientific uncertainty. This "wait and see" approach rests on optimism that climate disruption will not occur, or that market signals will somehow induce the appropriate responses.

A bolder approach is essential. If we wait for an elusive "certainty," we could well wait until it is too late. Postponing action would violate the precautionary principle, which requires anticipatory actions to ensure the well-being of future generations despite scientific uncertainty. The risk of severe and irreversible climate disruption demands immediate, forceful and sustained effort. Otherwise, we would continue to "lock in" production processes and transportation patterns that require inefficient use of fossil fuels.

> The risk of severe and irreversible climate disruption demands immediate, forceful and sustained effort.

There will be no transition to a stable climate without an energy transition — a massive transformation in how we produce and deliver light, heat and mechanical power. No viable long-term climate policy can avoid dramatic reductions in fossil fuel combustion. We need to develop and deploy efficient technologies and renewable energy, and adopt more resource sparing land use practices. The ubiquitous and voracious appetite of modern economies and lifestyles for fossil fuels makes this a formidable global challenge.

Climate protection is not the only issue driving the need for an energy transition. Since many nations rely on importation of increasingly scarce fossil fuels, economic stability and geopolitical security remain at risk. At the same time, there is the "other energy crisis," the unmet need for affordable and clean energy of the world's poor. Energy markets and governments have failed to provide household electricity and modern fuels to a billion poor. Meanwhile, dirty power plants, fumy vehicles and smoky coal furnaces and wood stoves foul the air — and lungs — in cities and rural households.

> An energy transition based on the twin pillars of renewable resources and energy efficiency would have numerous social, economic and environmental benefits.

An energy transition based on the twin pillars of renewable resources and energy efficiency would have numerous social, economic and environmental benefits. Energy efficiency would save the scarce economic resources of households, businesses and national treasuries, whose redirection would stimulate economic growth and job creation. Renewable energy could benefit economies and increase self-sufficiency. Climate policy could thus help to induce technological progress and spur productivity. These multiple potential benefits of carbon-reduction strategies thus redefine the challenge of climate protection. Rather than a drain on resources, climate protection is better viewed as a long-term societal investment with returns spread across the industrialized North and developing South, rich and poor, urban and rural.

Yet the goal of climate stabilization is daunting. For example, a commonly cited goal is to keep the atmospheric concentration of carbon dioxide below 450 parts per million (ppm). Many environmentalists consider this to be a weak constraint because this concentration would be so much greater than the pre-industrial level of 280 ppm. Nevertheless, a "450 World" would reduce the risk of large-scale climate, ecological and socio-economic

# THE CHALLENGE OF CLIMATE CHANGE

disruptions. But here's the rub — to meet that goal, global annual emissions, which could triple by the end of the century if no preventative measures are taken, would need instead to be more than halved.

The complexity and scope of the climate challenge require new global governance mechanisms that take an intergenerational, interdisciplinary and intergovernmental approach. The global community took the first step by establishing the 1992 United Nations Framework Convention on Climate Change, which set the goals and principles for coordinated international action. The 1997 Kyoto Protocol advanced the Convention by setting first phase goals for greenhouse gas emission reductions and providing mechanisms for compliance. If ratified, the Protocol would commit the industrialized world to reducing its annual greenhouse gas emissions to about five percent below 1990 levels by 2010.

> The climate challenge requires an intergenerational, interdisciplinary, and intergovernmental approach.

But many questions remain unresolved. The Protocol's mechanisms for providing industrialized countries with flexibility in meeting their targets are controversial — trading emission permits, taking credit for emission reductions from investments abroad, and planting forests as an offset to their emissions. To some, these mechanisms provide opportunities to meet targets more cost-effectively and to address ecological and social problems. However, if not used cautiously and sparingly, they are simply loopholes that enable wealthy countries to dodge their responsibilities and court ecological degradation and social disruption. The Kyoto "flexibility mechanisms" may have a valid niche in a climate arrangement, but should not detract from the fundamental obligation of industrial countries to reduce their own emissions.

An even greater barrier to ratification is the opposition of the United States, which has failed to provide global leadership on the climate issue. Rather than seizing the opportunity to decrease climate risks while modernizing the U.S. energy system and positioning the economy for the future, the stance of the current Administration is stunningly myopic. In addition to erroneous economic concerns, the U.S. objects that Kyoto does not require reductions from developing countries. It is true that the initial obligation falls on the industrialized countries in recognition of their historic responsibility for causing the problem and their economic capacity to address it. However, the climate convention also acknowledges the need for the eventual participation of developing countries in a "common but differentiated" framework, in order to achieve the necessary reductions over the twenty-first century. With only five percent of the world's population but almost twenty-five percent of its greenhouse gas emissions from energy use, the U.S. needs to take the lead in emission reductions along with other industrialized countries.

> The United States has failed to provide global leadership on the climate issue.

Kyoto is only a tentative first step on a long path. Its reduction targets are modest, measured against requirements to stabilize the global climate. The real value of the Protocol is that it begins the international climate negotiations process by demonstrating much of the industrialized world's commitment to climate protection. Without such a commitment, it would be difficult to justify the future involvement of the developing world.

In the long term, the success of international cooperation on

# THE CHALLENGE OF CLIMATE CHANGE

climate change rests on the pivotal question of equity. What is a fair recognition of rights and distribution of responsibilities for climate protection? Equity is a complex concept that involves consideration of fairness across income and social groups, businesses and workers, nations and communities. While the overall economics of climate protection can be positive, those facing near-term losses before adapting to the new policy and technology regimes deserve assistance in a just transition. In our polarized world, it is particularly critical that an international agreement on climate protection equitably assign rights and responsibilities to the North and South.

In retrospect, it is clear that the North has exploited much of the atmosphere's limited capacity to absorb greenhouse gases over its century of fossil-fueled economic growth. In doing so, the North has acquired the financial, technological and institutional resources to shift to the low-carbon path required for climate stabilization. The South, with economic growth and poverty alleviation its chief priorities, now finds itself in a world whose climate

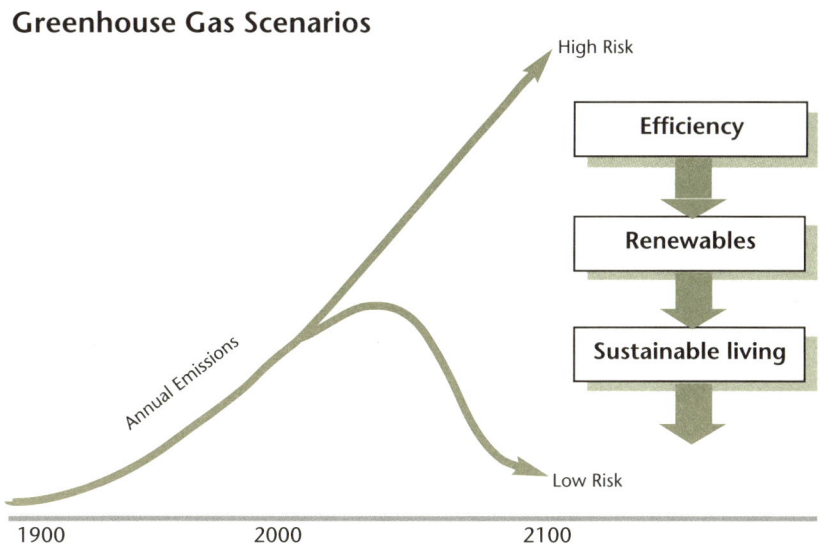

**Greenhouse Gas Scenarios**

system would be severely compromised if it were to follow the North along an energy-hungry fossil fueled path to affluence. Perversely, the South would more heavily bear the brunt of a changing climate. Desertification in Africa, flooding in South Asia, and the collapse of indigenous communities' forest habitats are some of the potential consequences for the South. The South faces a vexing dilemma — it must not replicate the environmentally dangerous path taken by the North, but it lacks the resources to forge a new development model.

> A good two-pronged approach is a constraint on global emissions and a path toward allocation of emission allowances among the nations of the world on an equal per-capita basis.

This situation places a special responsibility on the North to roll back its unacceptably high carbon emissions while assisting the South to transition onto a low-carbon development path. This would give room for emissions in the developing world to increase in the near term as their economies grow and as they transition to a low carbon future. Ethics and effectiveness require that the Climate Convention be structured to ensure a steady and rapid transition to a post-fossil world, based on adequacy for climate protection and equity in the allocation of responsibility for the necessary emissions reductions. A good two-pronged approach is, first, a constraint on global emissions that keeps greenhouse gas concentrations at no more that 450 ppm, and, second, a path toward allocation of emission allowances on an equal per-capita basis amongst the nations of the world.

The South's challenge is finding the economic resources for the transition to climate-friendly energy strategies, while at the same time attending to its pressing needs for poverty alleviation, adequate food, clean water, public health and human development.

Technology and financial transfers under the Climate Convention will need to support this broad agenda through win-win strategies that simultaneously diminish greenhouse gas emissions while fostering development. Equitable access to the Earth's atmosphere, such as the eventual convergence towards equal per-capita greenhouse emissions allowances, could help the South to earn the needed economic resources. The countries of the South could choose to sell underutilized emissions allowances to the North, thereby acquiring substantial revenues for investment in development along a sustainable path.

How these revenues are utilized is a matter of equity, empowerment and governance within each country. Public participation should be guaranteed, and principles to ensure ecological and social integrity should be established in international and national covenants on climate change. Correspondingly, efforts are needed to vastly expand and deepen human and institutional capacities for these tasks. Rising to this climate challenge would herald a new epoch in global governance, in which nations, communities and civil society play complementary roles, resting on the principles of democracy, equity and ecological resilience.

# Water in a Thirsty World

FRESHWATER IN SUFFIcient quantity and of adequate quality is critical to the health of people, economies and the environment. The aphorism "water is life" captures this essential role. As it courses through its grand hydrological cycle, water binds together the fates of nations with shared watersheds and river basins, and diverse users drawing from common water resources. It also links society with nature, for water is the lifeblood of ecosystems and the wider community of life.

Viewed from space, water would seem to be anything but scarce on this "blue planet." But most of it is in oceans and other saline water bodies. Only about 2.5 percent of global water is fresh — and most of that is frozen in glaciers and ice caps. Still, an immense amount of freshwater flows through the biosphere — 20 cubic meters per person each day, on average. That figure is misleadingly high, however. About 20 percent of freshwater resources are simply too remote for human use. Most of the water that is accessible is lost in floods, though dams help capture some of this. This means that about 6 cubic meters per person per day is reliably available on average.

On the demand side of the water balance equation, withdrawals for agriculture, households and industry average about 2 cubic meters per person per day. In addition, sufficient water must be left in the rivers for hydropower, for the dilution of pollutants to maintain adequate water quality, and for ecosystem protection. The combination of withdrawals and in-stream needs is over 3 cubic meters per person per day. Currently, then, global requirements are about half the available resources, certainly an uncomfortable margin when contemplating a future of growing water use.

Over the last century, the demand for water soared everywhere, driven by growing populations and economies. Globally, water withdrawals increased by a factor of seven during the twentieth century, almost twice as fast as the increase of population. A continuing planetary engineering project is creating a vast plumbing system of dams, diversions and waterway modification, transforming the world's rivers and the ecosystems that depend on them. At the same time, increasing pollution is contaminating rivers, lakes and underground aquifers. But freshwater is a finite and fragile resource. Increasing water use

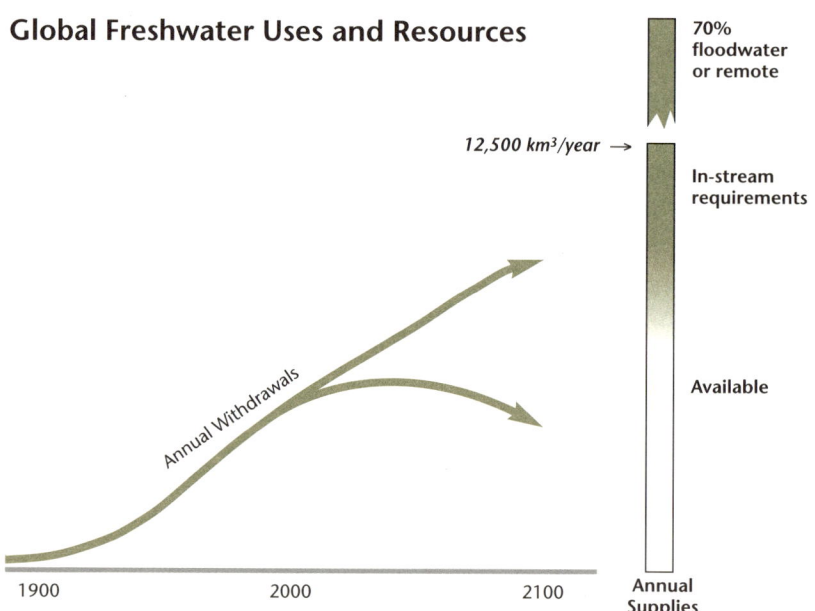

inevitably must collide with resource limits, jeopardizing economies, ecosystems and human health.

This global picture masks the huge variation across local river basins. In some places water is abundant — the ten wettest countries account for over half of water resources — while in many others there is dire scarcity. A more fine-grained picture reveals that some two billion people — one-third of the world's population — currently live under conditions of water stress. In these areas, available water is insufficient to satisfy all competing needs. A widespread symptom of water stress is over-pumping of water from beneath the Earth's surface, gradually exhausting and degrading groundwater aquifers that are slow to replenish and cleanse. In some places, a vicious cycle of water misuse and environmental impact amplifies the water dilemma. For example, inappropriate irrigation practices can cause the buildup of salts in soils, which, in turn, increases water requirements.

> Increasing water use inevitably must collide with resource limits, jeopardizing economies, ecosystems and human health.

Meanwhile, population and economic growth continues to drive water demand higher. Unless these trends change, billions more will be added to the ranks of people living in conditions of water stress. As water becomes scarce and degraded, conflict over its allocation among competing uses is unavoidable. In various regions of the world, the lines of conflict are drawn between farm and city, upstream and downstream users, and nations sharing common river basins. But one fissure is universal — the battle between water for human use and water for nature. In this competition, the environment is almost always the loser. The loss is measured in vanished wetlands, degraded riparian ecosystems and extinct freshwater species.

There is a second loser — the poor people throughout the developing world who lack basic water services. If the loss of aquatic ecosystems is an enduring tragedy of water mismanagement, preventable disease is a scandal of our time. Today over a billion people lack safe drinking water. Burgeoning urban populations in cities stress capacities to provide and distribute water, a problem already evident in metropolitan areas in developing nations. Degraded water supplies and exposure to pathogenic microbes pose severe threats to human health. The links between water quality, poverty and disease have been understood since the middle of the nineteenth century. Yet, to this day, three billion people do not have access to basic sanitation services, leading to some 250 million cases of waterborne diseases each year and over 5 million deaths.

> The cycle of poverty, insufficient water services and disease will persist until direct initiatives are taken to raise the living standards of the poor.

Economic growth alone will not eliminate this dire problem. Higher incomes will tend to gradually reduce poverty and increase expenditures for basic water services. But other factors — population growth, inequitable income distribution, and reduced water availability — will counteract the benefits of general economic growth. The cycle of poverty, insufficient water services and disease will persist until direct initiatives are taken to raise the living standards of the poor, provide modern water and sanitation services, and subsidize access to such services.

A vexing concern in many parts of the world is the competition between water for food and fiber, on the one hand, and for nature, on the other hand. Agricultural irrigation accounts for 70 percent of global withdrawals and dominates water budgets in many regions. In developing countries, rising populations and incomes will drive food demands substantially higher in the coming years. This will increase the pressure for water withdrawals for irrigation, as will agro-industrial initiatives vying for global export markets.

Competing demands for water for crops, for industrial and household uses, and for the environment will eventually require a reconsideration of economic development policy. In many countries, it will be difficult to maintain the conventional goal of food self-sufficiency and at the same time meet human and environmental water needs. Food imports, which indirectly "import" water, can reduce local water requirements for agriculture. But increasing food imports would require water-scarce countries to restructure their economies and to accept greater dependence on international food markets. Other areas, especially in the North, would need to expand food production to meet the increased demand. A global solution will require that developed regions respond with policies to meet global food needs at fair terms while addressing their own environmental agendas.

The multi-faceted freshwater crisis has crept up quietly and slowly. Other global issues have had their dramatic moments to galvanize public awareness — the energy shortages of the 1970s, the discovery of the stratospheric ozone hole in the 1980s and the warming weather of the 1990s. Compared with these issues, the water problem is more diffuse, chronic and gradual. Water was long the forgotten issue, rating nary a chapter in *Our Common Future*, the seminal 1987 report of the Brundtland Commission on global environmental concerns. That neglect has changed over the last decade as a series of international assessments, commissions and conferences has moved water higher on the global agenda. But the project of forging a path toward water sustainability — simultaneously meeting the needs for basic human services, economic demands and ecosystem preservation — has only begun.

How will we balance the numerous human and environmental claims on the Earth's finite freshwater? New sources of supply can help in niche situations. Desalination can contribute in some coastal cities if production costs continue to drop. Treated wastewater can be applied in certain agricultural settings. Rainwater harvesting, micro-dams and other traditional low-cost strategies can play a role. But on the negative side of the water balance sheet, supplies will be lost to the silting of dams and to the increased flooding anticipated from climate change. Ultimately, the gap between rising demands and limited resources will need to be closed through managing demand growth, reducing losses and protecting the environment.

Consensus has emerged on guidelines for action. A key dimension is the "ecological principle" — the recognition that the freshwater crisis is coupled strongly to a host of social and environmental concerns. In the past, water development was defined as a problem of engineering rather than ecology. But the challenge of water solutions that balance the needs of nature and society transcends engineering fixes. Another dam, levee or canal is no longer a sufficient answer. The traditional piecemeal engineering-based approach is now part of the problem. A new approach must be cultivated that casts the multiple dimensions of the water issue in a systemic framework in order to fashion comprehensive strategies. This will mean ultimately placing the water issue in the context of the larger debate on the character of development.

> A new approach must be cultivated that casts the multiple dimensions of the water issue in a systemic framework.

Complementing the ecological principle is the "institutional principle." The loci of decision-making should move from centralized political and administrative entities to the level of the river basin or aquifer. The many claims on water can best be recognized and appropriately adjudicated at these geographic scales. This strongly suggests the active participation in decision-making by those most directly affected by the outcome. Water sustainability will require balancing multiple interests and goals. The competing claims on limited water resources must be represented — sectoral demands, downstream users and the environment.

The active participation of stakeholders representing diverse perspectives, experiences and knowledge traditions is a pre-condition for fashioning broad-based and politically acceptable solutions. Government has the critical role of establishing the overarching principles, and creating the appropriate policy and management framework.

Water has been too long undervalued and underpriced. Water prices need to be guided by water costs — financial, environmental and social — in order to efficiently allocate supplies and encourage conservation. Widespread perverse price subsidies, such as for irrigation, encourage water overuse and undermine rational and equitable management. Without a price structure reflecting economic and environmental costs, the necessary investment capital will not be forthcoming, while nature's capital will be depleted.

Aligning water prices with costs is an important instrument for water policy. At the same time, governments must implement appropriate regulations to guarantee that water markets serve the larger objective of sustainability. In developing countries, this must include "virtuous" subsidies that ensure access to basic water and sanitation services to all. Ironically, in many places where water systems are dysfunctional, the poor, dependent on water middlemen, pay the highest prices. Government, the private sector and the research community must put renewed emphasis on the development and deployment of efficient and low-cost water technologies for meeting an array of local needs.

Gradually we have come to recognize the interplay among water, ecology and social justice. A global consensus is emerging on water strategies that recognize the rights of people today, of future generations, and of the larger web of life. A successful transition in the ways we use and appreciate water must be guided by the values of enhanced efficiency, distributive justice, and environmental integrity.

# The End of Waste

INDUSTRIAL ECONOMIES are like vast machines. Prodigious quantities of natural resources are fed into the system of production to yield an immense array of products. The flow of materials from the natural environment through to consumers is the very basis for economic activity. But, inevitably, material flows in reverse as well, from human enterprises back into the environment. At each step waste is generated as a by-product of human activity. The waste stream in pre-industrial times was a mere trickle. Today, fed by numerous tributaries with sources through-out the economy, this flow has grown to a roaring river comprising a complex brew of gaseous, liquid and solid wastes.

The most ubiquitous form is municipal waste — the plastics, metals, paper and garbage that course steadily from our homes and offices. Discarded computers, appliances and cars swell the waste stream. But the catalogue of waste includes huge quantities of less visible sources, as well. Massive amounts of residual material are left from mining operations. Fertilizers and pesticides are washed from agricultural fields. Liquid and sludge are discharged from factories and sewage treatment plants. At the point of consumption, countless chemicals, such as cadmium from tires and air emissions from autos, are released during product use and dispersed into the environment. More than 75,000 synthetic chemicals are fabricated, incorporated in products and ultimately released into the environment, although their impacts on human and ecosystem health are poorly understood.

The movement and chemical transformation of waste after the initial discharge to the environment further complicate the picture. Air pollution turns acidic and rains down on terrestrial ecosystems and human settlements. Pesticides applied to farmland percolate to underground water aquifers. Persistent organic pollutants accumulate in the food chain, reaching dangerous levels in fish products and even mothers' milk. Chemically active wastes react to form new substances. These transformations and synergies defy easy characterization, and they continue to challenge government regulators responsible for protecting human health and the environment.

> The movement and chemical transformation of waste after the initial discharge to the environment further complicate the picture.

Over half of all resource inputs are returned to the environment as waste materials each year. The most voracious consumer of materials in the world is the U.S., which annually generates nearly 1.5 tons of solid waste per person — far more than this if one includes indirect waste such as the overburden that collects at mining operations. The nation obtained most of its material requirements from organic and renewable resources at the turn of the twentieth-century, but gets three-fourths from non-renewable resources at the beginning of the twenty-first. Despite regulatory efforts at waste reduction, potentially hazardous wastes from all sources in the U.S. have doubled in the last twenty-five years. Burdens of this magnitude, testing the limits of natural systems to absorb and assimilate, cannot continue indefinitely without jeopardizing nature's life-support systems and courting ever intensifying human health risks.

While the industrial nations historically have dominated global waste generation, this likely will change over the coming decades. If the development path in poorer countries, home to 80 percent of the world's population, follows the consumption and production model of the industrial world, waste from developing nations will rise dramatically, eventually dwarfing levels in the industrialized countries. Already, emerging economies such as India, China, and Brazil are exceeding both natural waste assimilation capacities and government capabilities to regulate waste generation. In rapidly growing economies, most of the industrial facilities that will be operating in the next decade have not yet been built. If they replicate the waste-intensive technologies of industrialized countries, pollutant burdens will soar to unprecedented levels. The complex impacts on local, regional and even global environments would pose increasing perils to the environment and human health.

> If the development path in poorer countries follows the model of the industrial world, waste from developing nations will dwarf levels in the industrialized countries.

How can humanity improve the quality of life while reversing this seemingly inexorable rise in waste? What might a low-waste future look like?

Nature provides useful guidance. Over billions of years, nature evolved highly efficient solutions for processing and recycling materials in closed loops. It operates in a tightly integrated fashion, linking energy and materials in cycles of life-giving and life-sustaining functions. Natural systems are arranged in hierarchies. Biotic populations are parts of micro-ecologies, which are contained in complex ecosystems such as forests and wetlands — which together are part of the grand hydrologic, atmospheric and oceanic cycles. Materials unused or shed by one subsystem nourish another. This intricate fabric, woven over eons, is fraying in mere decades owing to the intrusion, burden and disruption caused by human generated waste.

Waste is a human invention, alien to natural systems. The key to ending waste is to transform the economic metaphor. If the industrial economy is like a machine that converts resources to products and waste in a linear chain, the sustainable economy of the future must be a web — like an ecosystem of cyclic material flows. The "waste" that is output from one activity must be used as input to another. Loops are closed, positive synergies are optimized, and the very idea of waste gives way to a new industrial ecology. Rather than a single approach, a bundle of reinforcing changes is needed in technology, product design, industrial structure and even consumption patterns. Together they go well beyond technical fixes to redefine how we produce and consume.

> The sustainable economy of the future must be like an ecosystem of cyclic material flows.

The phasing out of waste begins with radically decreasing the amount of virgin materials required as input to the economy and gradually substituting renewable resources, such as the many forms of biomass, for nonrenewable resources. The popular waste management mantra — reduce, re-use and recycle — embraces an immense range of options for decreasing material requirements per unit of product. Recycling at the end of a product's life — collecting and processing the paper, plastic and organic material in consumer garbage into a new cycle of resource inputs — is well known. Re-use strategies capture and refurbish such products as bottles, clothing, appliances and motors.

A less recognized but crucial point of intervention lies in the production phase where three factors are critical: the efficiency with which materials are used, the capture of waste as a raw material within the production system, and the design of products for re-capture and re-use. The term "eco-efficiency" has become shorthand for efforts by businesses to reduce the environmental burden for each product or service. At its simplest level, firms become more eco-efficient when they simply eliminate waste through better "housekeeping" and plant management. At the next stage, a business might invest in new processes, such as efficient chemical or steel manufacturing.

Eco-efficiency is the logical first line of attack in waste reduction. It speaks the language of business, and it is achievable here and now, as hundreds of companies and facilities have amply demonstrated. Efficiency, the inverse of waste, is a word all enterprises understand. The call for eco-efficiency can be squared with profitability — lower material and environmental control costs, reduced liability risk for environmental damage, and improvement in market niche afforded by a "green" image. Eco-efficiency can potentially reduce waste by perhaps a factor of five from current levels if the right mix of information, incentives and standards is put in place.

> Industrial systems can adapt nature's design principles so that waste is virtually erased.

But eco-efficiency alone is not sufficient for the needed industrial transformation. The economic and demographic drivers that are increasing waste volumes can only partially be offset by efficiency gains alone. In addition, we must adopt a systemic perspective on the entire industrial culture. The cradle-to-grave materials cycle must be recast into a cradle-to-rebirth mold. Industrial systems can adapt nature's design principles so that waste is virtually erased, and process and product design becomes based on "regenerative" rather than "depletive" principles.

In this vision of industrial ecology, the manufacturing process is analogous to living organisms with their own metabolism, with inputs of material and energy and discharge of wastes that are returned to the biosphere in degraded form. Materials are borrowed, not consumed, and wastes in one part of the system are redefined as food for another part. The energy lost in electricity production is captured for heating buildings and processing materials. The metals not used in one process become raw material inputs to another. While any component imperfectly converts material, the system as a whole has zero waste as its primary design objective.

> Smart product design can substitute information for materials while delivering superior function to businesses and household consumers.

Complementing eco-efficiency and industrial ecology is a third approach — the substitution of information for materials in the creation of value. This has the potential to drive "dematerialization" further, faster and deeper into the "genetic" structure of production systems. Smart product design can substitute information for materials, while delivering the same or superior function to businesses and household consumers. Some examples are: washing machines that electronically adjust water levels and temperature for load characteristics; onboard electronics designed to assist drivers in navigating the shortest distance to a destination or to continuously optimize fuel use according to road conditions; displacement of answering machines by call-answering services; and substitution of traditional phone lines with cellular technology.

While some dematerialization technologies appear to unequivocally reduce environmental impacts, others remain uncertain. Introducing engineered genetic material into natural systems may achieve efficiency gains in agriculture, but with a

## Closing the Material Cycle

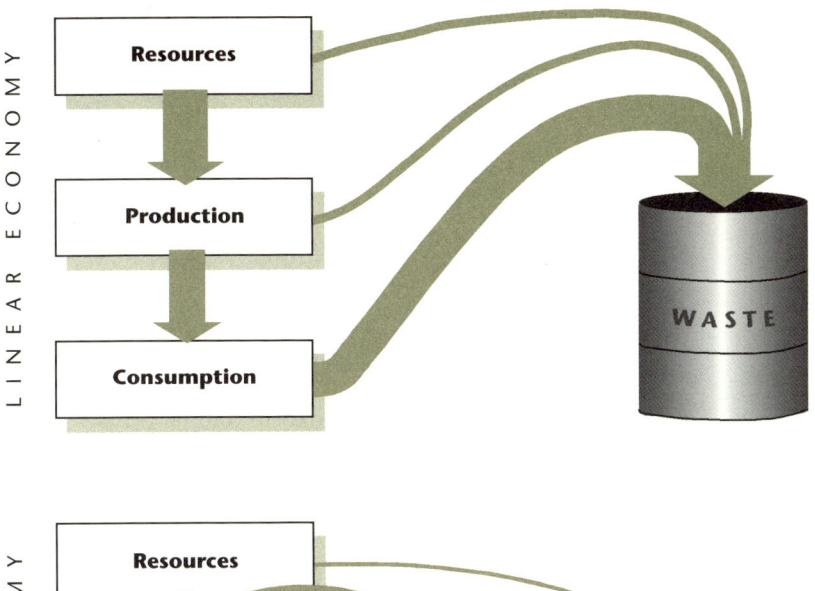

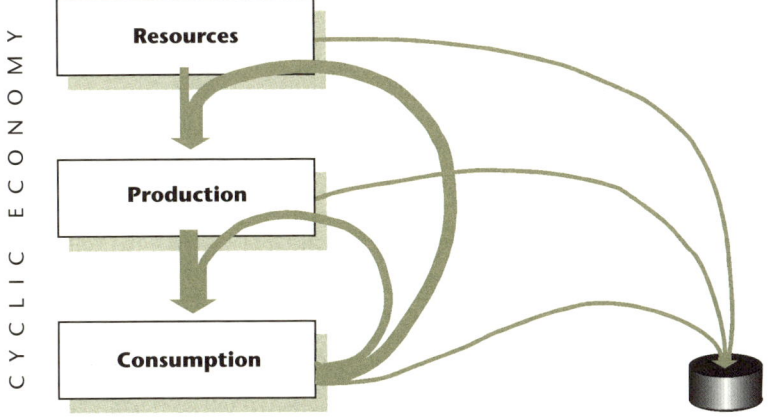

**LINEAR ECONOMY**

Resources → Production → Consumption → WASTE

**CYCLIC ECONOMY**

Resources → Production → Consumption

potential loss of biodiversity. Internet commerce has complex environmental implications as it alters packaging, transport, land-use and energy patterns. The challenge is to identify the opportunities for science and information technology to dematerialize economies, and to create policy incentives to hasten this transformation.

Today, perverse economic subsidies encourage raw material extraction such as timber extraction and oil drilling from public lands. At the same time, regulatory barriers sometimes discourage the use of recycled materials. Flawed national accounting systems treat environmental "bads" as economic "goods" that add to GDP. For example, the clean-up costs for contaminated land or the health costs resulting from poor environmental conditions contribute to "economic growth." These misleading signals reinforce the culture of waste and quietly undermine the principle of stewardship of natural capital.

> We must encourage, or mandate, materials stewardship in which producers take responsibility for the ultimate fate of their products.

Ending waste will require a comprehensive constellation of policies including regulation, incentives, research and collaborative partnerships involving the private sector, non-governmental organizations and government. We must encourage, or mandate, materials stewardship in which producers take responsibility for the ultimate fate of their products — appliance and auto take-back programs, tax incentives for leasing products rather than purchasing them, subsidies for remanufacturing used products. Certain materials that produce extremely hazardous wastes, such as mercury and persistent organic pollutants, should be phased out or highly restricted.

These strategies — more efficient technological systems, the re-use of materials and products, and the substitution of knowledge and information for materials — have huge potential to reduce waste. But, even if they begin to reduce the material flow, increasing consumption keeps driving it up. If consumerism persists in the wealthy countries, the expansion of the economy will counteract improvements in the efficiency of production. If Western lifestyles and values define the development model for a

## CLOSING THE MATERIAL CYCLE

world of twice today's population, the scale of human activity could increase by another factor of ten in the coming decades.

Unbridled consumerism must give way eventually to less materially oriented lifestyles that value quality over quantity and community over consumption — once a comfortable level of material well-being is achieved for all. We begin with waste, a seemingly prosaic matter, and come to fundamental questions about the way we live and produce. The view of the Earth as a bottomless sink for waste, a harmless misunderstanding when the human footprint was small, has become a dangerous myth. Ending waste is a commitment to tomorrow.

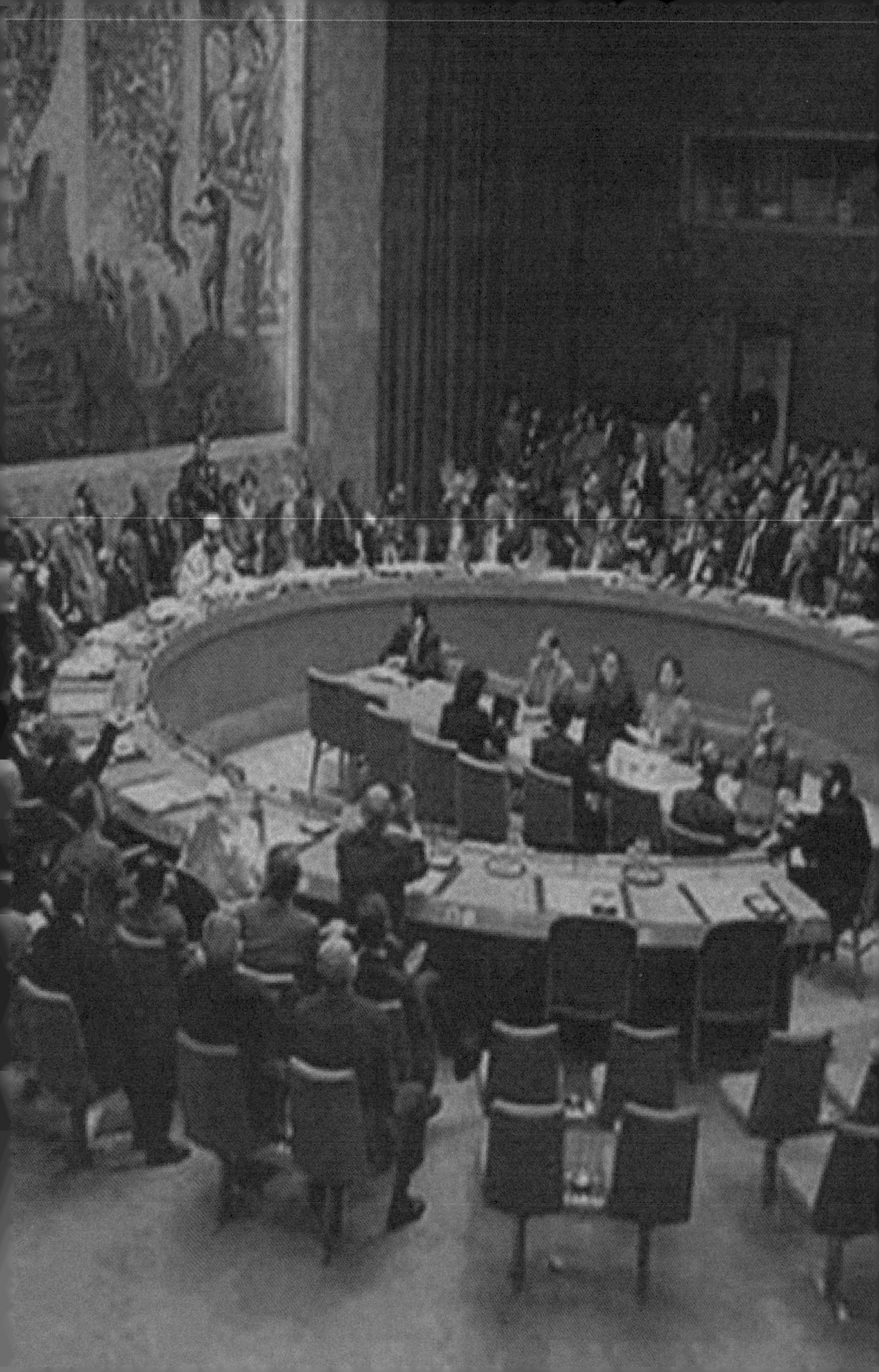

# Sustainability and the New Agenda

IN 1992, THE UNITED Nations organized the Earth Summit in Rio de Janeiro. Its aim was to highlight concerns about the global environment and development, and to galvanize international action. The nations of the world responded by adopting sustainable development as a guiding policy principle. This new paradigm calls for harmonizing economic growth with ecological constraints, and for eradicating poverty. Sustainable forms of development seek to provide for the people of today while passing on an undiminished world to future generations.

The rhetoric of Rio has not been converted into much action. The sustainability challenge requires a long-range perspective, systemic thinking and integrated policy. Yet national leaders tend to be responsive to a myopic and fragmented set of political and economic interests. As the ten-year anniversary of the Earth Summit approaches, the juggernaut of market-driven globalization rolls on, with little sign of reversing either environmental stress or human deprivation.

Nonetheless, the quest for sustainability animates growing global initiatives of non-governmental organizations, countless individuals, forward-looking businesses and governmental agencies, and has begun to enter the discourse of political parties. This nascent movement has broadened the debate on development, providing a counterweight to the values of consumerism and growth-for-growth's-sake that underlie conventional development thinking.

Sustainability is ultimately an expression of humanity's deepest collective ethical values. To advocate sustainability is to appreciate and respect the interdependence of the world's people, of humanity and the biosphere, and of the present and future. It compels us to take responsibility for the well being of others, the resilience of the Earth system and the future. It requires us to give voice to the voiceless — the poor of today, the wider community of life, and the unborn of tomorrow.

> Environment, economy and equity are understood as aspects of a unitary global project for a livable future, requiring systemic rather than piecemeal strategies.

Sustainability reflects the basic aspirations of our historic moment — ecological integrity, quality of life and social justice. Environment, economy and equity are understood as aspects of a unitary global project for a livable future, requiring systemic rather than piecemeal strategies. The sustainability framework sees environmental health as a precondition for a viable economy, not merely an "externality" requiring marginal adjustments and technical fixes. In the past, environmental policy has often been reactive, relying on end-of-pipe technology. The new paradigm calls attention to possibilities for building environmental protection into the design of production processes and eco-efficient economies — clean energy sources, not just better smokestacks, and product re-use, not just safe disposal. For many, the sustainability idea stimulates a reconsideration of the meaning of the good life, so long equated with higher levels of material consumption.

Combining poverty elimination with environmental health is a practical necessity as well as an ethical imperative. Poverty is both a cause and an effect of environmental degradation. It is a cause since concern about environmental preservation is a luxury that desperate people cannot afford. It is an effect because the global poor suffer most from the dislocations of ecological disruption. So land-hungry people are pressed to convert ecologically valuable forests for subsistence farming, then see their livelihoods threatened when the land becomes degraded through unsustainable agricultural practices. All the while, the world grows less equitable, not more. Global income quintupled in the last fifty years, but the benefits accrued disproportionately to the rich — the income of the richest 20 percent was thirty times the income of the poorest 20 percent, but is now eighty times. Extreme poverty and inequality undermine the long time horizons and social cohesion necessary for tackling the sustainability

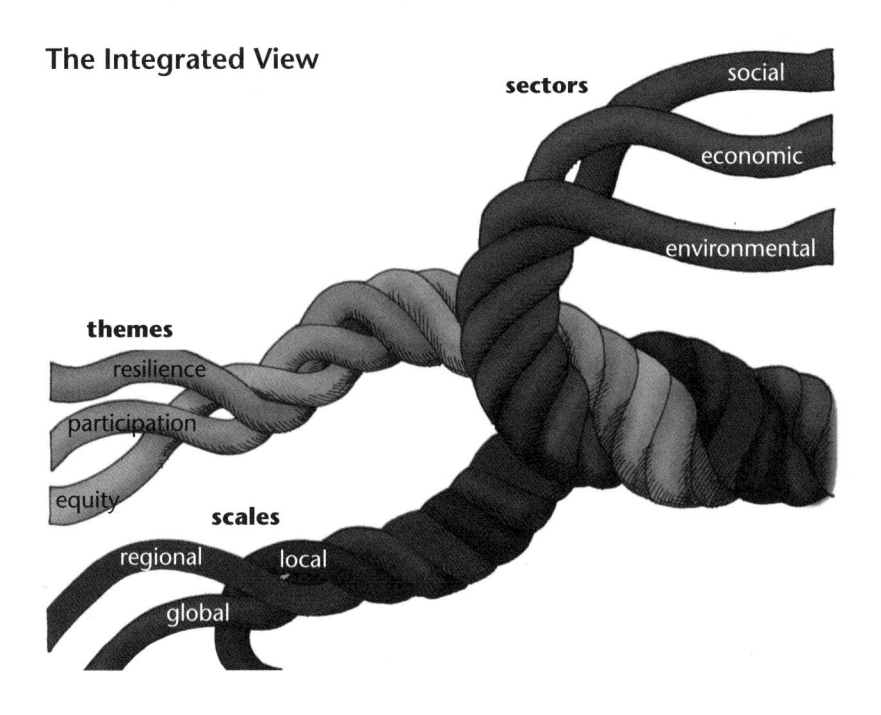

**The Integrated View**

sectors: social, economic, environmental

themes: resilience, participation, equity

scales: regional, local, global

challenge. Eliminating them must be part of the transition to sustainable development.

Sustainability poses fundamental challenges to science and policy. The essence of sustainable development is the harmonization of human activity and ecological preservation. This is only possible with an integrated perspective that blends social, economic and environmental issues, and transcends the conventional practice of decomposing both nature and society into their constituents. Policies must address simultaneously the goals of social equity and ecological resilience, and do so at global, national and regional levels. If nurtured, the critical dimensions of sustainability — systemic knowledge, new values and integrated action — can reinforce one another in a process of social transformation.

> Governance patterns, the myriad ways in which collective decisions are made, must evolve to meet the challenges of sustainability.

Governance patterns, the myriad ways in which collective decisions are made, must evolve to meet the challenges of sustainability. Good governance means the ability of a collectivity to make informed choices that are both legitimate and sustainable. But traditional governmental institutions seem swept along in the frenetic tide of globalization, while new forms of governance, such as the World Trade Organization, accelerate rather than mitigate the adverse consequences of globalization.

How can the pursuit of environmental stewardship and poverty reduction be built into governance structures? Rigid and universal formulas are not useful. Effective and appropriate institutional responses are likely to be diverse, adaptive and democratic.

While some over-arching governance is essential, it should be minimized. In order to encourage participation and match

## SUSTAINABILITY AND THE NEW AGENDA

solutions to local circumstance, decision-making is best retained at the smallest appropriate scale. Such "subsidiarity" would be conditional, however, since in a governance system for sustainability, higher scale environmental and social goals must act as constraints. For example, national energy systems would be diverse, but subject to greenhouse gas emissions constraints set by global agreements. Local water strategies would vary, but must be compatible with allocation rules and ecosystem goals set at the river basin level. Trans-national issues, affecting environment, commerce, peace, migration, and technology transfer, will require effective global governance mechanisms. In the planetary phase, global governance structures must emerge to coordinate the interdependent affairs of nations, just as nation-states once coalesced from fragmented city-states. The United Nations could play an important role if empowered and restructured as the locus for global decision making.

> Information technology provides the communication medium for expanding networks, building public awareness and intervening in international negotiations.

An important new force for effective governance has entered the global stage to shape environmental, labor, human rights, and development agendas. Civil society, impatient with the sluggish response of governments to environmental threats and concerned about growth in corporate power, has spawned numerous non-governmental organizations of unprecedented sophistication, reach and influence. Information technology provides the communication medium for expanding networks, building public awareness and intervening in international meetings and negotiations. Many corporations have felt pressure from international groups, which use codes of conduct, consumer boycotts, public disclosure, and direct action to get global corporations to behave as global citizens.

An innovative form of governance is multi-stakeholder initiatives, including working groups of governmental agencies, non-governmental organizations and businesses. These collaborative networks have sought common approaches for such issues as corruption, dam construction, land mines, corporate disclosure and sustainable forestry. One process, the Global Reporting Initiative, is working to fashion broad standards for corporate behavior and for reporting transparent information on corporate performance. This novel approach will likely be important in specific niches of the global economy. But its role in the transition to sustainability will be successful to the degree it is enforced by civil society as watchdog, by government as enabler and regulator, by markets that reflect environmental costs, and by citizens as ethical consumers.

> A new cluster of initiatives at the local level offers a fresh approach to promoting sustainable livelihoods.

New governance structures will be needed to address the concerns of the poor. National governments are largely unresponsive to politically marginalized communities. Multilateral lending agencies and the WTO focus on the stimulation of private investment and aggregate economic growth, rather than the needs of those at the bottom of the income ladder or outside the formal economy altogether. But a new cluster of initiatives at the local level offers a fresh approach to promoting sustainable livelihoods. These efforts are highly diverse, while sharing a commitment to grassroots participation, providing the poor with access to capital, and deploying appropriate technology. By asking, not what the poor need, but what the poor can do to cope with their situation, they strengthen existing individual and collective capacities rather than importing solutions. They emphasize sustainable management of local natural resources by the local communities that value and depend on them. Finally, they enhance the resilience of communities to deal with future shocks, whether environmental, economic or political.

The transition to a sustainable planetary civilization requires a sea change in policy, governance and technology. This is surely an awesome challenge. But this revision of how we conduct our affairs must rest ultimately on a still more fundamental modification in what we believe and the way we live. Only a change of awareness and popular values can drive the politics of sustainability. A planetary civilization shaped by consumerism, individualism and greed cannot resolve the environmental perils and heal the social fissures that it creates.

The quest for a better quality of life, not simply a greater quantity of things, will need to inspire individual endeavors. This will mean a search for lifestyles that are materially sufficient, and rich in meaning and fulfillment. Appreciation of being part of a grand planetary web-of-life can inspire a sense of awe. Awareness of shared global destiny can awaken a feeling of human solidarity based on compassion, diversity and respect.

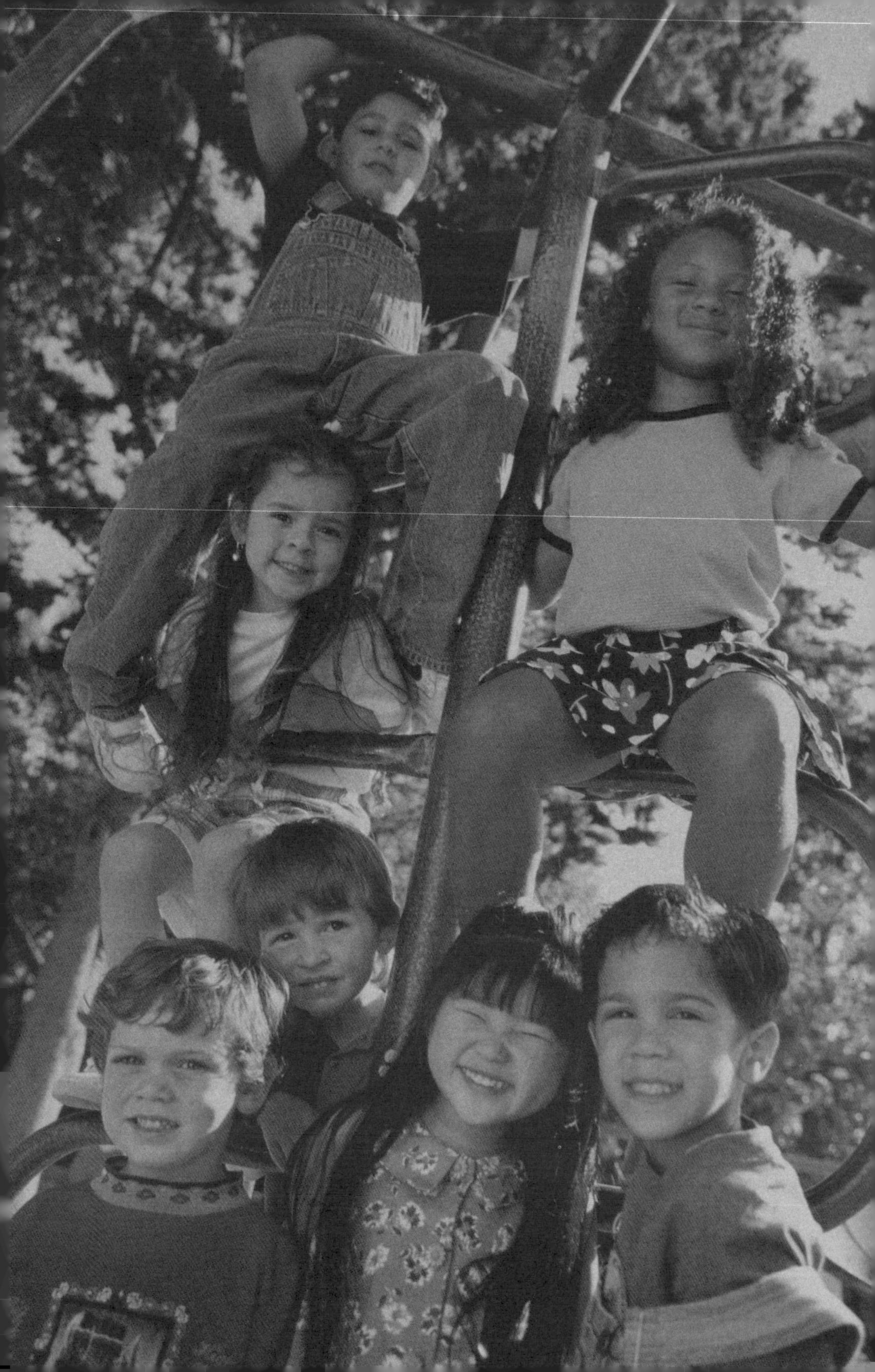

# Our Grandchildren's Bequest

HUMANITY IS CONDUCTING a vast experiment in rapid global change. What kind of world will result? We cannot know with certainty. What we do know is that planetary transformation poses a deeply troubling proposition — the burden of unsustainable development today will be borne by our grandchildren tomorrow. Concern for human destiny and the fate of the Earth, once the domain of dreamers and visionaries, has become a moral and practical imperative for all. The question of the future moves to the mainstream of public policy, scientific research and the popular imagination.

While we cannot predict the global future, we can scan the broad possibilities. Consider three scenarios for the twenty-first century — *Conventional Worlds, Fortress Worlds and Great Transitions. Conventional Worlds* evolve gradually, governed by today's dominant values and trends. *Fortress Worlds* depict futures, perhaps nascent in these trends, in which crisis, conflict and environmental degradation lead to a degeneration of civilization. *Great Transitions* are responses to the sustainability challenge based on new values and humanistic forms of social and economic organization.

Market-driven development is the essence of *Conventional Worlds*. In such futures, transnational corporations are increas-

## Global Futures

ingly dominant as free trade agreements and unregulated capital and financial flows spur economic globalization. The values of consumerism and individualism spread. Most developing regions slowly converge toward the consumption and production patterns of the rich countries. Information technology accelerates the process of globalization. Cultural diversity diminishes in the march toward a world society. Traditionalist and fundamentalist backlash flare up, but are contained.

By 2050, global population grows from 6 billion to 9 billion, with all of the increase in developing countries. The scale of the world economy soars more than fourfold. Environmental pressures grow more severe as the increasing scale of human activity overwhelms gradual improvements in the resource efficiency of technology. While economies grow everywhere, so does inequality between and within countries. Absolute global poverty persists, as increased population and greater income inequality counteract the poverty-reducing effects of economic growth.

How are the environmental degradation and social tension of *Conventional Worlds* resolved? As the scenario unfolds, many are complacent, trusting competitive markets to eventually reverse environmental degradation through the self-correcting logic of prices and innovation, while wealth eventually trickles down to the poor. Others are less sanguine, advocating a policy reform agenda — comprehensive action to sustain the environment and reduce poverty in the spirit of the Brundtland report and the Earth Summit. The policy reform agenda does not challenge the dominant institutions, values or basic development model of *Conventional Worlds*. Rather, it calls for improvements in technology, technological transfer to poor regions and international programs to eliminate poverty.

> There is no absence of means to achieve sustainability, but a paucity of political will within the conventional development paradigm.

Achieving sustainability in the context of the rapid economic growth of *Conventional Worlds* is daunting. Nevertheless, a vast repertoire of technical options is potentially available for eco-efficient production, poverty elimination and sustainable livelihoods, and an arsenal of policy instruments could accelerate these changes. There is no absence of means to achieve these goals, but a paucity of political will within the conventional development paradigm. The challenge for sustainability within *Conventional Worlds* futures would be to transcend the inertia of institutions, the myopia of political leaders and the resistance of entrenched interests.

If a politics of sustainability does not succeed in the context of market-driven global development, ecological and social stress could spiral out of control and global development could veer toward a *Fortress World*. In this dark vision, governments gradually retreat from social concerns, development aid declines and poverty rises. The global poor are reached not by economic development but by the global media. Tantalized by images of opulence and dreams of affluence, the excluded billions grow restive. Many attempt to migrate to wealthy countries, where the response is increasing xenophobia and police protection. The poison of social polarization grows more virulent. Deteriorating environmental conditions, growing food insecurity and spreading disease accelerate the crisis. In this atmosphere, violence spreads, feeding off old ethnic, religious and nationalist tensions. Poor countries begin to fragment as civil order collapses and various forms of criminal anarchy fill the vacuum.

The richer nations also feel the sting. The global economy sputters, international institutions weaken and climate change takes its toll. With the global dispossessed clamoring at their borders and terrorism and disease spreading, the affluent fear that they too will be engulfed by a crisis that seems to be spinning out of control. In this atmosphere, global forces — transnational corporations, international organizations and armed forces — react with sufficient cohesion to impose order. In the *Fortress World* that arises, the wealthy protect themselves in enclaves within rich nations and strongholds within poor nations. The fortresses are globally connected islands of privilege amidst oceans of misery in which the majority is mired in poverty and denied basic freedoms. Police measures control social unrest, prevent migration and protect the environment. An authoritarian form of "sustainable development" is imposed.

Such a grim future is possible but by no means inevitable. The sense of peril and the appeal of forging a new development model could trigger a very different response to the sustainability challenge. A civilization could emerge based on the values of respect for the community of life, global solidarity and concern for the well being of future generations. In the *Great Transition*, a new international politics appears, stimulated by concern over the erosion of planetary ecosystems, public health and humane values. The conviction spreads that the weakening of governance systems, begun in the late twentieth century, must be reversed.

> In the Great Transition, a new international politics appears, stimulated by concern over the erosion of planetary ecosystems, public health and humane values.

The global movement for a new development paradigm has a powerful personal and philosophical dimension — a search for more fulfilling and ethical lifestyles. The values of simplicity, cooperation and community begin to moderate those of consumerism, competition and individualism. Voluntary reduction in work hours frees time for study, art and hobbies. Lifestyles become simpler materially and richer qualitatively as the obsession with things gives way to intellectual and artistic pursuits. Youth from all regions and cultures rediscover idealism as they join together in forging a planetary community. The Internet is the natural medium for an expanding and pluralistic global network to advance the new agenda.

Measures of development success increasingly focus on equity and quality of life, rather than the narrow metric of economic growth. Gradually, the new sustainability paradigm finds expression in a growing number of communities that opt for alternative lifestyles and economic practices. Urban life is slowly reshaped around integrated settlement patterns that place home, work, commerce and leisure activity in closer proximity. As dependence on the automobile abates, a sense of community cohesion is established. For many, the town-within-the-city provides the ideal balance of a human scale with cosmopolitan cultural intensity. Others find dispersed small towns attractive as communication and information technology increasingly allow for the decentralization of activities.

> Economic activity is constrained to be compatible with social, cultural and environmental goals.

In the *Great Transition*, markets remain indispensable for achieving efficiency in the allocation of resources. But economic activity is constrained to be compatible with social, cultural and environmental goals. This is enforced both by policies — regulation, standards, public projects, negotiation, and revised tax systems — and by a vigilant public that shuns the products of offending businesses. Forward-looking corporations, prompted by reaffirmation of corporate citizenship through new charters and codes of conduct, advance a new ethic based on meeting human needs instead of multiplying human wants. A universal system of environmental accounting — in which pollution and resource depletion count as economic losses rather than gain — is integrated with indices of development to provide a better signal of economic performance. In this context, an explosion of technology innovation accelerates the sustainability transition.

The environment gradually heals as the material flows through the global economy begin to decrease. De-materialization results from rapid population stabilization and a swift transition to renewable resources and eco-efficient technology. But it is driven by an important third factor — the displacement of consumerism by the ethos of material sufficiency. While the material economy stabilizes, development flourishes in the non-material realm of services, culture, art, sports and research. At the same time, a labor-intensive craft economy rises spontaneously on the platform of the high technology base, providing a rewarding outlet for creative expression and a proliferation of highly aesthetic goods and services. Demand for locally grown and environmentally friendly food spurs a new generation of farmers to develop agricultural practices based on low input of chemicals and high input of ecological science.

Governance evolves toward a nested system in which regions and communities have considerable control over socio-economic decisions and environmental preservation at the local level. But they must conform to constraints imposed by governance of higher-level political systems. Global governance relies on a rejuvenated United Nations to express the politics of diversity-through-global-unity of *Great Transitions*. A sustained international mobilization for education, economic opportunity and poverty reduction begins to redress long-standing inequities within and between countries, while speeding the stabilization of populations. A growing peace dividend helps support the program of environmental and social renewal as national defense systems are dismantled gradually.

At the middle of the twenty-first century, the *Great Transition* does not fulfill the millennial dreams of its more utopian early advocates. Pockets of poverty remain, geopolitical conflicts still flare up, environmental and resource problems require continued attention, and life's personal conflicts and tragedies remain. Yet the world community takes great pride in its immense achievements in human development, global solidarity and eco-

> While the material economy stabilizes, development flourishes in the non-material realm of services, culture, art, sports and research.

logical renewal. A new generation looks forward to the challenge of forging a sustainable civilization of creativity, freedom and shared destiny.

If we could survey the social-scape of many decades from now, what would we find? We might discover a *Conventional World* that felt familiar, once we became acclimated to an astonishing set of new technologies and commodities. Or would we be horrified to see that after a time of chaos, a *Fortress World* emerged from the ashes of the industrial era? Or perhaps we would find that our descendants had shed the shackles of our historical imagination in a *Great Transition* to fashion a global civilization of unprecedented humanity, fulfillment and justice.

> Global development can come to embrace ecology and justice, or veer toward degradation and conflict.

The drama of global transition has begun. Though we can observe its early scenes and gauge the arc of its narrative, the full story is not yet written. One thing is certain. The contradiction between the growth imperative of conventional development and a finite planet will be resolved. But will it be through the incremental adaptations within *Conventional Worlds*, the calamity of *Fortress Worlds*, or the renewal of *Great Transitions*? Global development can come to embrace ecology and justice, or veer toward degradation and conflict.

In the theater of history we are actors who have the freedom to shape the future into tragedy, farce or the stuff of dreams. We have the good fortune to live at a critical time in which our actions can influence the world our children and grandchildren will inherit. It is this conviction and this challenge that must animate our work and our lives, now and in the decisive decades ahead.

# Acknowledgments

Paul Raskin, President of Tellus Institute, Steve Bernow and Allen White, Vice Presidents, comprised the core writing team for this essay. Senior staff at the Institute drafted material on various topics — Tariq Banuri, Sivan Kartha, Michael Lazarus, David Nichols, Ken Strzepek, and John Stutz — or offered useful comments — James Goldstein, Jeanne Herb, Annette Huber-Lee, Paul Ligon, David McAnulty, Richard Rosen, Deborah Savage, and Karen Shapiro. We wish to thank Faye Camardo and Ross Gelbspan for editorial inputs and Jack Sieber for electronic wizardry.

The scenarios of the future are based on the Global Scenario Group's *Branch Points: Global Futures and Human Choice,* which Paul Raskin co-authored (http://www.gsg.org). Raskin has elaborated these scenarios further for the United Nations Environment Programme's third *Global Environment Outlook* report (2001).

Tellus has worked with thousands of collaborators, partners and sponsors throughout the world over the last twenty-five years. Although far too numerous to name here, we wish to thank them for the support and wisdom that has enabled Tellus to evolve with the times to become the organization that it is today. We hope that this essay provides a provocative basis for continued co-evolution in our common future.

1976

+25
Back row: John Stutz, David McAnulty, Paul Raskin.
Front row: David Nichols, Richard Rosen, Stephen Bernow.

# About the Tellus Institute

The name Tellus refers to the Roman goddess of the Earth who attended to the earth's well-being and productivity. Two themes — environmental stewardship and equitable development — lie at the core of the vision of sustainability and at the heart of the mission of the Tellus Institute.

Founded in 1976 as a nonprofit research and policy organization, Tellus addresses a broad range of environment and resource issues. The Institute's staff of fifty scientists and policy analysts is active throughout North America and the world. Internationally, Tellus works closely with the Stockholm Environment Institute, hosting SEI's Boston Center since 1989.

The transition to a sustainable world must occur at many levels. Tellus contributes to this goal through its work on global scenarios, regional and national strategies, community sustainability and industrial ecology. Projects focus on such areas as energy, water, waste, transportation, and integrated sustainability planning. The Institute's diverse sponsors — foundations, governments, multilateral organizations, non-governmental organizations and business — reflect this varied program.

Tellus is a leader in the development of appropriate methods for analyzing complex problems and guiding effective solutions. It disseminates decision-support tools and software to strengthen the capacity of governments, NGOs and citizens for integrated environmental and development decision-making.